First published in Australia in 2026 by Affirm Press,
a Simon & Schuster (Australia) Pty Limited company
Wurundjeri Woiwurrung Country
Level 3, 162 Collins Street, Melbourne VIC 3000
Affirm Press is located on the unceded land of the Wurundjeri Woiwurrung peoples
of the Kulin Nation. Affirm Press pays respect to their Elders past and present.

New York Amsterdam/Antwerp London Toronto Sydney/Melbourne New Delhi
Visit our website at www.simonandschuster.com.au

10 9 8 7 6 5 4 3 2 1

A catalogue record for this
book is available from the
National Library of Australia

9781923293199 (hardback)

Cover and interior design by Andy Warren Design
Printed and bound in China by RR Donnelley Asia

INCLUSION

ZANNI LOUISE
ART BY JINGTING WANG

A NOTE TO BIG HUMANS:

Thank you for choosing this book. This guide will help you chat with the little humans in your life about what it means to be **inclusive**.

Read this book together. Ask questions, listen and share. This guide is designed to be a conversation starter and a book that little humans can look at any time they need.

If you have questions, come by and see me at www.zannilouise.com.

Your friend,

Zanni

INCLUSION
#3

Being a human isn't always easy.

There are so many things to learn, like:

- brushing your teeth
- your left and right
- how to sign your name.

Here's another thing to add to your list: **being inclusive.**

What does that mean? Good question! Being inclusive is when we make the world feel friendly and safe for everyone. Shall we take a look?

WHAT IS INCLUSION?

Have you ever changed your game so everyone can play?

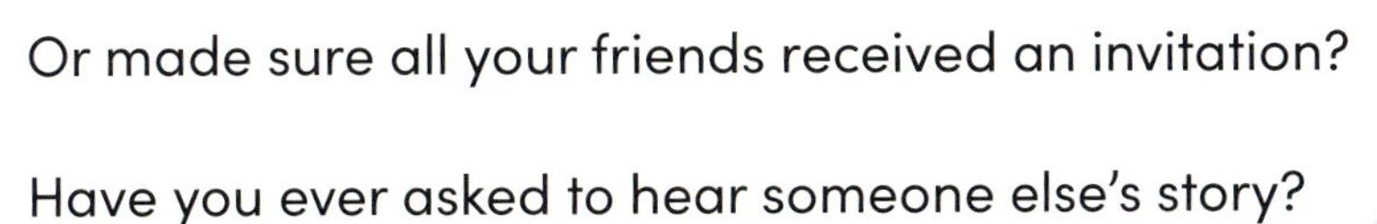

Or made sure all your friends received an invitation?

Have you ever asked to hear someone else's story?

I bet that's because you were **being inclusive**. When we're inclusive, we do our best to make everyone feel welcome, no matter who they are. That way, everyone gets to join in and have fun.

HUMANS ARE ALL DIFFERENT

Imagine a world where everyone looks, dresses, sounds and thinks the same. It sounds a bit like Robot Land. Beep-beep-boooooring!

Luckily, humans aren't robots. We're different in all kinds of ways: age, gender, race, culture, language, ability, strengths, tastes, sock choices ... I bet you can think of other ways we're different too.

Robots might all like the same game and have the same needs. But not us humans. We are *way* more interesting than that.

We don't always understand each other's differences. But that's okay. We have time to learn.

RIBBIT
HEY
WOOF
CHIRP
BEEP
HI!
TOOT!
HELLO!
BUZZ
AH

LISTEN AND LEARN

I don't know about you, but when I meet a new person, I feel **curious**.

I want to know who they are and how they see the world.

The more I learn, the bigger my heart and mind grows.

When you meet someone new, you might like to ask them questions and listen to their story. It's like opening a door to a whole new world.

BEING PROUD OF WHO YOU ARE

So, little robot (I mean, *human*), let's talk about what makes you unique.

Can you think of something you're proud of? Is it your hair? Your superhuman chilli-eating ability? How fast you can count to one hundred? The way your family celebrate birthdays?

Maybe it's the fact that you're a nice person most of the time.

Being proud of yourself is important. So is supporting other people to feel proud of themselves.

THERE'S A LOT WE SHARE

Being unique is excellent. But being different from each other shouldn't mean someone misses out, right?

Sometimes, though, our differences make it hard to join in.

Luckily, there's something we all share – **feelings**. That's why we all know what it's like to feel sad when we're left out.

Here's a tip: imagine how your friends are feeling and think about ways you can include them.

The next story might help.

Yummy, yummy!
Ooh, bananas!
Come up!
Have some with us.
These bananas are so good, Fox.
I'm scared of heights.
I can't.

We'll come to you.
Wow ... Really?
Bananas taste better with everyone, don't you think?
You'd be bananas not to share with all your friends!

HELPING EVERYONE FEEL WELCOME

People feel left out for all kinds of reasons. We might not mean to leave someone out. It can happen accidentally. We might just be too busy focusing on our game!

It helps to pay attention. And if someone seems sad, do what you can to make them feel included. It might simply be a smile. Or a wave. Or you can respectfully ask them what they need.

YOU BELONG TOO

One last thing, my friend. If you ever feel like you're on the outside, I want you to remember that **you belong**: in your home, with your family, with your friends, in your community.

If there's something you need, don't be afraid to speak up and let someone know. Just as you make others feel included, you deserve to feel welcome too.

WHAT DID WE LEARN ABOUT INCLUSION?

Humans are different in so many ways. But we all love to belong and feel welcome.

Including others is great for everyone, including you! You get to learn new things, and your heart and mind grow. So does your world.

When we make an effort to check that everyone can join in, we have more friends to play with and the world is a happier place.

So, Little Human, you can learn lots of things, like:

- ✓ brushing your teeth
- ✓ your left and right
- ✓ signing your name.

And now, you can add being inclusive to your list too! Have fun, my friend, and make sure that your friends are having fun as well.

✓ **INCLUSION**